I WANT TO BE A
CIVIL ENGINEER

Written & storyboarded by
Jonathan Reule

Illustration
Phan Quỳnh Trang

UNIBINO
BOOKS

First paperback edition May 2023
ISBN 978-981-18-6520-6

Published by Unibino Pte. Ltd.
31 Rochester Drive Level 3, #03-47 Singapore 138637

www.unibino.com

Civil engineers are like the backbone of modern society. They have helped us escape nomadic lifestyles and brought us into bright and vibrant cities. But it hasn't always been this way.

In fact, hundreds to thousands of years ago, humans mostly lived out of tents, moving from place to place, following animals to wherever they may roam. Thanks to civil engineers, we eventually managed to build permanent homes and cities so we no longer had to move around.

When we think about modern cities, what comes to mind are sprawling bridges, tall towers, robust railway systems, and even mighty harbours where boats from all over the world can dock. But did you know that we haven't always had such structures?

Long ago, the technology used to build buildings was not as advanced, and many buildings crumbled only a few years after their construction. Even worse, they were no match for the natural disasters that often struck without warning.

This is how civil engineering came about. We had to figure out how to fortify and protect our homes and cities so that they wouldn't be destroyed by the forces of nature so easily. For example, the people of ancient Jordan built one of the oldest known dams, the Jawa Dam, to help prevent flash floods from creeping into their towns and destroying their crops.

The ancient Egyptians often suffered from famine due to prolonged droughts which resulted in a severe lack of food. To overcome this, they used civil engineering to build massive granaries to store extra food during prosperous times so that they could survive periods of famine.

A great breakthrough in civil engineering came about in the 3rd Century BC when Archimedes, a dedicated inventor, applied his mathematical abilities to industrial designs. One of his most significant contributions is the pulley, which allows us to lift heavy objects that might be impossible to carry.

Archimedes is also renowned for his study of fluids at rest. This has helped physicists and engineers build bridges over water sources, as it is crucial for them to understand how flowing water impacts the foundation of a bridge.

The ancient Romans also made significant contributions to the field of civil engineering. They had a deep understanding of engineering principles and built giant aqueducts that allowed clean water to flow from lakes and seas straight into their town centres.

Even to this day, the grid designs used by the ancient Romans can be found in most modern cities. So the next time you're driving downtown, try and observe the layout of your city — they could have been inspired by ancient Roman cities.

Romanesque architecture remained the standard for buildings and engineers for centuries until new techniques were developed in mediaeval France — bringing us into what is known as the Gothic period.

With this advancement in engineering techniques, we could make towers taller, walls stronger, and buildings larger in size thanks to these three main principles: the Flying Buttress, Ribbed Vault, and the Pointed Arch.

FLYING BUTTRESS

RIBBED VAULT

POINTED ARCH

We certainly have come a long way since the Gothic period, and without these fundamentals, we would not have been able to build the great structures you see today in our modern world. Thanks to the Romans, we are able to build harbours and roads to travel upon.

We've also benefited from French engineering allowing us to scale our skyscrapers high up into the sky. What's more, did you know that in Japan, there are skyscrapers that can withstand high-magnitude earthquakes? Talk about a giant leap in progress for civil engineers.

The Coffee House

Now you might wonder, what does it take to become a civil engineer? For a start, you will need to be able to think outside of the box and be able to apply your learnings in mathematics and physics to your designs.

You will also need to be able to think outside of the box and work towards finding solutions to seemingly impossible situations. Take the Channel Tunnel (Chunnel), for example, an undersea tunnel that connects England to France. The engineers had to think of creative solutions to build the tunnel when many believed it was impossible.

Next, it's good to know what type of civil engineer you'd like to be, as there are several different areas of specialisation you can explore.

Environmental engineers use their scientific knowledge to help create healthier environmental conditions. They may suggest plants in certain areas to manage erosion or even desalination solutions to help irrigate crops.

Environmental engineers also strive to keep the air clean by finding ways to reduce pollution around the world.

Infrastructure engineers work with structures such as trains, railway tracks, roads and bridges that allow us to travel around. They play a crucial role in city planning, especially when designing connectivity for new neighbourhoods.

Geotechnical engineers work with soil and rocks to ensure that buildings or other structures are built on solid foundations before construction starts. They may also be hired to maintain or construct new dams.

Transportation engineers are in charge of building transit systems that keep our world connected. For example, they help to design and oversee the construction of airports, so aeroplanes have enough runway space to take off and land safely. They also work to develop underground subway systems, which are crucial, especially for large cities.

Structural engineers design buildings and other structures that need to withstand the forces of nature. For example, a structural engineer can help to construct a bridge over a wide river. It is essential that the engineers understand the long-term effects that the water has on the material of the bridge.

After deciding what type of civil engineer you want to be, it is time to plan your educational route. To get hired as a civil engineer, most companies around the world would require you to have at least a Bachelor's degree in a relevant field. For example, if you want to be a geotechnical engineer, you can consider a degree in geology and take physics and engineering classes at the same time.

Many civil engineers further their education by obtaining a Master's degree in their field of interest. This is also a good way for someone with an engineering or similar science degree to pivot into civil engineering after college.

Once you have completed the required education, it is time to apply for a job where you can use your knowledge in real-world situations. One of the best ways to do that is by starting at a junior-level position under a senior engineer who can also act as your mentor during your first few years.

Most importantly, you'll need to keep an open mind as you test and apply your ideas to real-world situations. If an idea does not work, try not to give up but instead approach the problem from another angle.

FUN WORLD

STOP

While you are working, it is vital to keep your end goal in mind. As civil engineers usually work on large projects that can take years to complete, it's good to keep in mind the reason you chose to be a civil engineer in the first place.

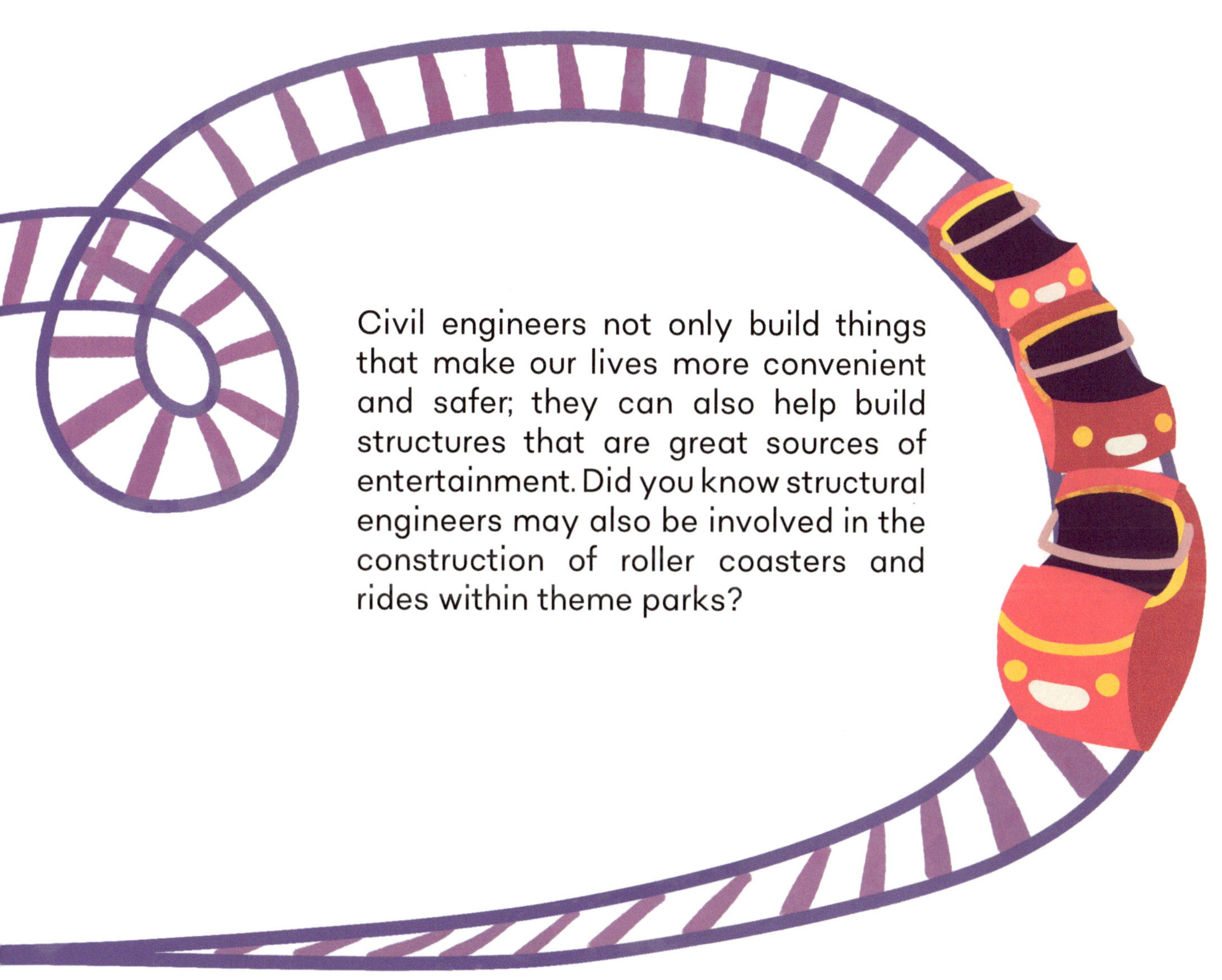

Civil engineers not only build things that make our lives more convenient and safer; they can also help build structures that are great sources of entertainment. Did you know structural engineers may also be involved in the construction of roller coasters and rides within theme parks?

So the next time you ride through a windy mountain road to a getaway retreat or travel over a bridge to a sunny beach island, it's good to remember that we are able to enjoy such conveniences thanks to civil engineers. Many things that we take for granted, such as roads or train tracks, were once planned out and designed by an engineer.

And who knows what the future might bring? How our natural environment will change, or how the buildings we live in might look in a few hundred years?

But if you continue to learn and attempt what others deem impossible, who knows what you might be able to achieve!

No matter how big or small your goals are, we will always need civil engineers to solve the tricky problems that come with living in our modern world. Perhaps even more so in the future!

My Inspiration

Shubhi Saxena
Founder, Unibino

As a parent in this ever-changing world, it can sometimes feel overwhelming when it comes to our children's futures. New technologies seem to be arising almost every day, and with so many innovations, it creates unique professions which many of us wouldn't have dreamed to be necessary only a few years ago. Which to me is a good thing. Because with so much variety, my children can have the opportunity to pick a career that will fit their personalities and build upon their strengths. As you may imagine, this desire within me to provide my children with the resources they needed to thrive, led me to search out books that would be easy enough for them to understand while teaching them about various professions.

Only, I found that these books were few and far between. Even if I could find a book about a certain profession geared towards young readers, I found them sparse inside and limited to only certain careers that may not fit my children's abilities. This is when I came up with the idea to write my own children's books, teaching them about all the various careers in the modern world. After months of researching different professions and learning more than I ever expected, I quickly realised this was going to be a bigger project than I first anticipated. I dove into the histories of these professions, discovering links to the past, and why these professions were now so important.

Ultimately my goal was to offer my children options, to show them that there is no one set path for everyone. But in this, I stumbled upon something bigger. I wanted to share this with future generations. To share with all children and parents about these careers, to help spark curiosity, and to instil a passion for the future. Everyone has special talents and abilities, and I hope that this series will be able to offer clarity and inspiration to children around the world. Because at the end of the day, it's never too early to start dreaming and never too late to take action. With this, I hope you enjoy this series and that your young ones become the best versions of themselves as they can achieve.